Bedtime Stories
for
Privileged Children

Bedtime Stories
for
Privileged Children

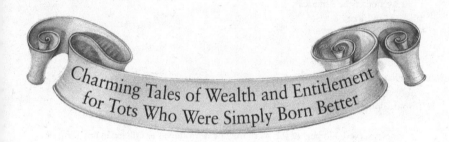

Charming Tales of Wealth and Entitlement
for Tots Who Were Simply Born Better

DANIEL FOXX

Illustrated by Axana Zasorina

monoray

First published in Great Britain in 2024 by Monoray, an imprint of
Octopus Publishing Group Ltd
Carmelite House
50 Victoria Embankment
London EC4Y 0DZ
www.octopusbooks.co.uk

An Hachette UK Company
www.hachette.co.uk
www.octopusbooksusa.com

Distributed in the US by
Hachette Book Group
1290 Avenue of the Americas
4th and 5th Floors
New York, NY 10104

Distributed in Canada by
Canadian Manda Group
664 Annette St.
Toronto, Ontario, Canada M6S 2C8

ISBN 978-1-80096-209-5

A CIP catalogue record for this book is available from the British Library.

Printed and bound in Canada

10 9 8 7 6 5 4

This FSC® label means that materials used for the
product have been responsibly sourced.

To John Lewis,

Without whom none of this would be possible.

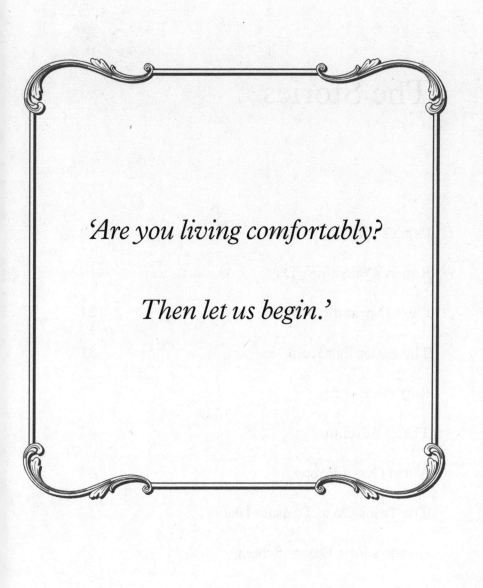

'Are you living comfortably?

Then let us begin.'

The Stories

Jasper's Birthday

'Wake up everybody!' cried Jasper, throwing on his Ralph Lauren quarter zip.

'It's my birthday!'

'Happy birthday, Jasper,' yawned Nanny 3, who had been up all night managing one of Mama's breakdowns.

Jasper loved birthdays.

He opened some presents, and played with his property portfolio, and made the staff carry him from room to room.

'I *never* walk on my birthday!' he laughed, waving his whip.

Then he opened his presents from Mama and Papa.

'An apartment block in Abu Dhabi! That will provide *excellent* returns!' said Jasper, who was eight.

It wasn't long before Jasper's friends started arriving for the BIG party. Perrier had brought him a whippet, whilst his friend Cholera brought him some culturally appropriated antiques.

Everyone had lots of fun at the party.

They rode their horses, and listened to a private performance by Rufus Wainwright, and Mama and Papa even pretended to love each other for the day!

Then they played musical chairs.

They went round and round, whilst the Berlin Philarmonic played in the background.

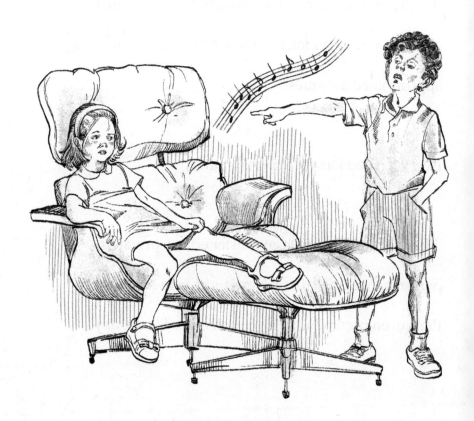

At one point, Cholera threw herself onto

an Eames chair whilst the orchestra was still playing.

'Disqualified!' laughed Jasper. 'They were playing

a *pianissimo,* not a *caesura!*'

Everyone found that *very* funny.

However, even though Papa had paid everyone to let

Jasper win, he ended up only coming *third.*

Jasper was very upset.

'Don't worry, Jasper,' said Nanny 2. 'I know what will cheer you up.'

'A return to classical ideals in modern Western architecture?' he sobbed.

'No,' chuckled Nanny 2.

'Giving some of these presents to charity!'

'...What on earth is *charity*?' said Jasper, gagging.

And he fired her on the spot.

She was right, though, he thought.

That did cheer him up.

Rupert's Valentine's Day

'**G**uess what, everyone?' cried Rupert. 'It's Valentine's Day!'

'Happy Valentine's Day,' said Mama, who was busy taking Ozempic.

Everyone *loved* Valentine's Day.

Rupert liked to dress up as a cherub and hunt the servants with a bow and arrow, and Chef would draw a special little heart on his macchiato. Mama and Papa even paused their affairs for the day!

This year, Papa gave Mama some blood diamonds, whilst Mama promised that later on, she would dress up as Papa's big celebrity crush: Theresa May.

Even Nanny 2 was getting into the spirit!

'Guess what my husband bought me, Rupert?' she asked.

'Oh, um, I don't know,' said Rupert, eyeing her

doubtfully. 'Something polyester…?'

'No,' she laughed, 'he bought me a weekend away

in **BLACKPOOL**!'

Rupert looked puzzled. 'Does he hate you, then?'

Later that day, Rupert met up with his good friends Arugula and Cremant. They ate lots of sweets and played some fun Valentine's games.

'Arugula, why don't you marry Rupert,' said Cremant. 'Nanny 3 can play the priest, and I'll be the lawyer who draws up the prenups!'

'That's a **wonderful** idea,' said Rupert.

'And then afterwards, I can push you down the stairs

and take all the money for myself!' said Arugula,

excitedly. 'Just like *my* mummy did!'

They thought that was **great** fun.

On the way home, Nanny 2 looked troubled.

'Oh Rupert, I'm very bad with presents,' she said.

'And I still haven't got anything for my husband!

What shall I do?'

Rupert thought long and hard about this. 'I suppose,

if you *really* wanted to treat him,' he said, slowly,

'you could pluck your moustache?'

And as Nanny 2's eyes welled up with gratitude,

Rupert skipped off down the street.

It was another *great* Valentine's Day.

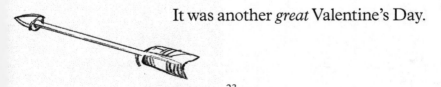

Lily's Day at the Office

———

'Come on, Lily!' said Papa, picking up his Hermès holdall. 'It's Bring Your Daughter to Work Day!'

'I think I'd better take that to go,' said Lily to Nanny 1, who was preparing her overnight oats, and they headed off to **The Conglomerate**.

Lily was excited.

'I'm wearing my new tweed power shoulders,' she said.

'So I see!' said Papa.

'And I'm going to pretend this sherbet is cocaine!'

'You'll fit right in,' said Papa.

There were lots of fun things to do at **The Conglomerate**.

Lily stapled the papers and arranged the Fiji waters,

then had a quick networking lunch with Kate From

Marketing.

'Thank you for a lovely lunch,' said Lily. 'We should go riding some time!'

'Oh, I don't have a horse,' said Kate From Marketing.

'That's okay,' said Lily. 'You can borrow one of mine!'

After lunch, Lily was very busy. She had to put away the mugs and colour in a picture of the company logo with crayons.

'Don't talk to me, I'm slammed,'

she snapped at anyone who would listen.

Then she had to shadow Stephen From Legal.

'So *Pauline* is sleeping with *Martin*, but *she* doesn't know that *Martin* is in love with *Derek*?' she whispered.

'That's right,' whispered Stephen From Legal, who lived for the drama.

Later that afternoon, Lily sat in on one of Papa's meetings, in which he was letting Sue From Accounts go.

'Perhaps you should have spent less time on maternity leave and more time being good at your job!' contributed Lily.

'That was a very good point, Lily,' said Papa in the

Mercedes on the way home, and they stopped off for

a couple of macchiatos.

It was the perfect end to a perfect day.

The Easter Egg Hunt

———

'He's been, he's been!' cried Hyacinth, admiring her new Fabergé egg. **'The Easter Bunny has been!'**

'Happy Easter, Hyacinth,' yawned Mama, who was enjoying a breakfast of muesli and uppers.

Hyacinth *loved* Easter.

Every year, she threw a big party and invited all her friends. This year, she was going for a *pagan* theme, and she decorated the whole house with help from the nannies and her two best friends, Cholera and Boursin. There were flowers and bunting, and a person in a giant rabbit costume.

'Who's in that rabbit, Hyacinth?' asked Boursin.

'Oh,' said Hyacinth, sadly. 'That's Alicia Keys.'

When the rest of the guests arrived, everyone got stuck into the party. They did some colouring, and danced around the garden, and sacrificed Nanny 3 on a limestone tablet. Then everyone did an Easter egg hunt.

'I've found one!' cried Cholera.

'I've got two!' said Boursin.

'You're legally obligated to let me win!' smiled Hyacinth, nodding at her lawyer.

It was a LOT of fun. However, halfway through the hunt, disaster struck. Boursin's mother discovered that there had been a mix-up with the Fortnum's order.

'Stop!' she screamed. 'Stop! This cocoa isn't **single origin**!'

Once the children's stomachs had been pumped and
everyone had signed an NDA, they all settled back down
on the picnic blankets with Olives and Parma Ham
– two of Hyacinth's other friends, who had arrived late.

To cheer them up, Mama gave each of the children a sip

of her Special Easter Punch, and told them the story of

Jesus' Trial and the Cross. She was very good at reading,

and did all the voices.

'So, there you have it,' she smiled, as the children swayed

gently on the lawn.

'The true lesson of Easter…

… always settle out of court.'

Rupert's Holiday

'Come on, Rupert!' said Papa. 'We're going on holiday!'

'Coming, Papa!' said Rupert, finishing up his ceremonial matcha, and they all piled into the Land Rover Defender.

When they got to the airport, Nanny 3 checked in everyone's Louis Vuitton monograms, whilst Rupert and Mama decided to explore.

'Can I have my pocket money for the duty free?' asked Rupert.

'Of course,' slurred Mama, passing him the Amex Black.

Rupert had *lots* of fun at the duty free. He bought a book about managing your trust fund and practiced his French with the ladies at Yves Saint Laurent, then watched the normal people sampling perfumes they couldn't *possibly* afford.

Soon it was time to board the aeroplane. Rupert, Mama and Papa turned **left**, but Rupert noticed

some people were being directed *right*.

'What's down there?' he whispered, looking at the cloth divider.

'Jealousy,' murmured Mama.

When they touched down, everyone began their holiday.

Papa dialled into a call with **The Conglomerate** and

Mama conducted an emotional affair with the concierge,

whilst Rupert and Nanny 2 went to take intrusive photos of the locals.

'Why are they putting their clothes in the water?' he wondered.

'They're *washing* them,' explained Nanny 2. 'It's a way of wearing clothes more than once!'

'*Gosh*,' said Rupert.

In the evening, everyone met back at the hotel for a light supper of tartines and prescription medication. They were having such a lovely time that they didn't even notice a hungry little orphan boy approach.

'Excuse me,' said the little boy. 'I'm terribly hungry. Could you possibly spare some money, or perhaps a little food?'

'...No, fuck off.' said Rupert, and they *laughed,*

and laughed,   and *laughed.*

It was the perfect holiday.

Theo's Adventure

———

'Goodbye Mama,' said Theo, picking up his Jacquemus Chiquito.

'I'm going on an adventure!'

'That's nice, Theo,' said Mama, who was busy signing her divorce papers.

Theo picked a direction and set off to explore.

He was going to be a real discoverer, just like his Grandpapa, who had discovered subprime mortgage loans!

Theo walked

    and walked,

        and before long he was in a new part of town.

The people were dressed differently here, and some of the houses were only semi-detached.

He took out his sketchbook to make a few drawings. He drew a pigeon, and a syringe, and a Renault Clio.

Theo felt like a true explorer!

Before long, he started to get hungry, so he headed into

a nearby bistro.

'Excuse me,' he asked. 'Have you any patisserie?'

'No,' smiled the man behind the counter. 'We only serve *chips*!'

Theo **ran** and **ran**, as fast as his patent leather brogues

could carry him.

Now he was truly lost! There were no boutique shops
at all here, and hardly a labrador in sight.

He stopped a kindly-looking woman.

'Pardon me,' he said, 'but what *is* this place?'

'Why, this is an estate, my dear,' said the kindly-looking
woman.

'Oh,' said Theo, hopefully. 'Are the Lord and Lady in?'

'You look hungry,' said the woman, and offered him
a packet of store-brand crisps.

It was at this moment Theo knew he was in **serious trouble**, and he pressed his panic alarm.

Within seconds, Nanny 2 and Security Guard arrived to whisk him back to The Townhouse.

'*The crisps,*' he whispered. '*They ... they were Aldi.*'

'Don't think about it, Theo,' murmured Nanny 2, stroking his hair. And they *sped off* to therapy.

Theo decided that, on reflection, maybe he wasn't the adventuring type after all!

Astrid Gets a Puppy

—

'Come downstairs, Astrid,' called Papa. 'I have a surprise for you!'

'Coming, Papa!' said Astrid, finishing up her earthenware, and she hurried down the stairs.

Down in the spare hallway, Papa was holding a big box. Astrid gasped.

'Is it my order of Augustinus Bader serums?' she said.

'No,' Papa laughed, and put the box on the floor.

The box seemed to be moving! It scratched, then it wobbled, then it let out a little **bark**.

Papa took off the lid…

…and out came a puppy!

'This is your new dog, Astrid,' said Papa. 'You have to feed her, and walk her, and pick up her mess.'

'But I don't even do those things for **myself**!'
Astrid wailed.

Astrid was nonplussed. She stomped back upstairs to her room.

'I don't want a dog,' she huffed. 'I want radiant pores!'

There was a chewing sound from below her bed. She looked down to see the puppy gnawing on one of her Aesop soaps.

'That one's for guests,' said Astrid, gloomily. 'I actually think there are higher-quality brands for personal use, although I'll concede I like their hand creams.'

She rolled her eyes. 'Come on then, Aesop,' she said. 'Let's get you some lunch.'

Astrid thought Aesop was *very* annoying. She put down a bowl of ceviche and a glass of dry white – but Aesop just stole one of Papa's venison steaks!

Then she took Aesop outside to look at her Zen garden, but Aesop just wanted to roll around in the mud!

'No, Aesop!' cried Astrid, as the puppy rubbed mud all over Mama's daybed. **'That's a Louis XV!'**

'We have *nothing* in common,' sighed Astrid later to Nanny 2, who was making her a coffee. 'She's loud, she doesn't ski, and she has only a limited grasp of Mandarin.'

'I'm sure you'll grow to love each other, Astrid,' said Nanny 2, passing her a cortado with oat milk. 'These things just take time.'

Just then, Aesop came barrelling into the room.

When she saw Nanny 2, she stopped in her tracks.

'**Bark, bark!**' said Aesop.

'What is it, Aesop?' said Astrid.

Everyone came running to see what was the matter.

'**Bark, bark!**' said Aesop.

She **barked** at Nanny 2, and she **barked** at Gardener!
She didn't bark at Mama, or at the photograph of Camilla
Parker Bowles, but she *did* bark at Security Guard 6.

Astrid gasped.

'She doesn't like poor people!' she said. 'We *do* have something in common!'

And from that moment on, they were the best of friends.

The Twins Go to
Treasure Island

'Land ho!' cried Priscilla.

'Drop the anchor!' cried Millicent, waving her

Hermès cutlass.

It was a bright, sunny morning and the twins were

playing pirates. They had put on pirate hats, and found

pirate swords, and borrowed daddy's yacht for the day.

The twins had even managed to buy an

endangered species of parrot on the black market!

It was lots of fun.

'Walk the plank, ye scurvy dog!'

said Priscilla, pushing Nanny 2 into the water.

'AHHHHHHPRISCILLANOICAN'TSWIM,'

said Nanny 2.

'What shall we do now?' said Millicent, once they got

bored of stamping on Nanny 2's fingers as she tried

to climb back on board.

'I know!' said Priscilla. 'Let's go to the beach and explore!'

They hopped into the rowboat and waited for Nanny 2

to paddle them ashore.

'Row! Row!' shrieked Millicent, helpfully.

There was lots to do on the shore. They looked in

the rockpools, and threw stones at the waves, and built

a sandcastle.

'It looks like the Monaco house!' said Priscilla.

Whilst they were playing, a bottle washed up on

the beach. There was a paper scroll inside!

'A map!' said Millicent.

'With a note!' said Priscilla.

'*The gold is hidden where no one can find it,*' read Millicent. 'Just like Daddy's offshore accounts!'

'It's a treasure map,' said Priscilla. 'Now we're real pirates!'

The map took them through many dangerous places.

They climbed a steep cliff...

Crossed a rickety bridge...

Walked through a local Lidl...

'I'm scared,' said Priscilla, crouching near the imitation breakfast cereals.

'Don't speak,' said Millicent, grimly. 'Just *run!*'

Eventually the map took them to a big empty cave where X marked the spot, and Nanny 2 started digging with her bare hands.

'I hope it's diamonds!' said Priscilla.

'I hope it's Bitcoin!' said Millicent.

But the twins didn't notice two scary men sneaking up on them. They were big and frightening, and one of them wore an eyepatch.

'Give us the treasure!' said the two scary men. 'Or else!'

'Real pirates!' said Millicent, who was scared.

Thankfully, Priscilla had remembered to bring Mama's

taser, and put the men into a mild coma.

The twins gathered round eagerly to see what Nanny 2 had uncovered. It was a big wooden chest, and when they opened it, it was full of gold and silver!

'Wow!' said the twins, picking up some of the jewellery.

'...Oh, it's Pandora,' said Millicent, dropping it hurriedly.

'Yuck,' said Priscilla.

And they put the treasure back in the hole. Still, thought the twins, they'd had quite the adventure!

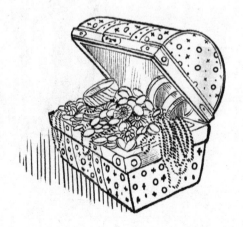

Cosmo's First Day
of School

———

It was Cosmo's first day of school, and he was *very* excited. Mama had driven him to the gates herself, and Papa's secretary had even sent a text to say good luck!

'Goodbye, Mama!' cried Cosmo, as they pulled up outside the big concrete building. 'I love you very much!'

'See you at Christmassss,' said Mama, who was late for Pilates – and she sped off in the Discovery.

Cosmo picked up his suitcases and headed inside. The school looked very different from the brochure.

'I suppose they've decided to go for a Brutalist aesthetic,' he mused.

He followed the other children inside. There was LOTS to do on their first day! They picked their desks, and introduced themselves to the class, and said what their parents did for a living. One girl said her mummy was a 'cashier', which Cosmo thought sounded *very* exotic.

'My daddy is a custodian of the family seat!' said Cosmo.

'That's not a job,' said a boy.

Cosmo thought that was *rude*.

At lunchtime, the children explored the grounds.

They ran around on the tarmac, and played a game called

'football', which is like polo without the horses, and

Cosmo got told off for being bossy to a member of staff.

He was *very* upset.

'I didn't know she was a teacher,' he sniffed.

'She was wearing jeans!'

Then they went to the canteen.

'Excuse me,' he asked a kindly-looking lady. 'Where is the **cheese** and **wine**?'

The kindly-looking lady laughed. Cosmo was confused. 'We do a different themed meal every Monday,' said the lady. 'Can you guess what this week's theme is?'

Cosmo looked at the food. '...Prison?' he asked, politely.

After lunch, the children had to write a short story about their summer holidays. Cosmo wrote his in Latin, but the teacher said that was wrong.

'I **hate** to be vulgar,' Cosmo said, 'but how much do I need to pay to be in the *good* class?'

'Don't be silly,' the teacher chuckled, patting Cosmo's head. 'This school is free!'

'Oh how *wonderful*,' smiled Cosmo, pressing his panic alarm.

'I'm *so* sorry, Cosmo,' said Nanny 3, as she rappelled

through the second-floor window moments later.

'You're in the **wrong school!**'

'Don't worry,' said Cosmo, 'I'm sure it's nothing valium can't fix.'

And they soared away in the helicopter.

Tarquin's Day at the Park

———

'**F**arewell, Papa,' said Tarquin, slipping on his Bottega cropped puffer.

'I'm going to the park!'

'Hmnmh,' said Papa, who was busy embezzling funds.

The park was very busy. There were people jogging, and nannies bitching about their bosses, and children flying big colourful kites.

'My kite is a dragon!' said a little girl.

'My kite is Emirates First Class!' said another.

Tarquin and his friends had *lots* of fun at the park.

They *swung* on the swings,

and d$_u$g in the sandpit,

and pretended the climbing frame was Soho House.

'Don't climb too high, Tarquin!' laughed Nanny 2.

'**You** can't tell **me** what to do,' laughed Tarquin, climbing higher. 'I'm your **employer**!'

'Ha^{ha}ha_{ha}ha,' laughed Nanny 2, imagining what it would be like to murder him.

Then Tarquin spotted another little boy sitting all alone on a bench.

'*Bonjour, je m'appelle Tarquin!*' he said. '*Je ne t'ai jamais vu ici – où vas-tu à l'école?*'

'Sorry, I don't speak French,' said the little boy.

'Oh, how *funny*,' said Tarquin. 'Then how do you ski?'

'I don't ski,' said the little boy.

Tarquin threw up in his mouth!

Later on, Tarquin and some of the other children decided to play a game.

'Why don't we play tag?' said one.

'Or hopscotch?' said another.

'I have an idea,' said a third. 'We should play horse racing!'

'But our horses are in the country!' said the little girl.

'Not to worry,' said Tarquin, 'our **nannies** can be

the horses!'

Before long they were all having the best of fun, sitting

on their nannies' backs as they crawled along the wet

grass. Tarquin even managed to get second place!

'Did you have a good time at the park?' panted Nanny 2,

covered in mud, as they walked home later.

'I did!' said Tarquin. 'But you lost that race for me,

so don't bother coming into work tomorrow.'

Camilla's Day at the Beach

'Bon voyage, tout le monde!' cried Camilla, grabbing her Prada raffia tote.

'I'm going to the beach!'

'Have fun, Charlotte,' murmured Mama, who was having her morning wine.

Camilla had lots of fun at the beach.

She painted a landscape and collected flat stones

to throw at the poor children, then paid a visit to

the ice cream van.

'One yuzu sorbet, please!' said Camilla.

'What about a 99?' said the man. 'It's traditional,

and only costs 99 pence.'

'What is a pence?' said Camilla, backing away hurriedly. After that, Camilla and Nanny 2 went to admire the beach huts along the coast.

'Look at the huts, Camilla,' said Nanny 2. 'Aren't they tiny!'

'Gosh, yes,' said Camilla. 'They look just like your house!'

'When I was a little girl,' said Nanny 2, wistfully, 'I used to come down to this beach every day and read my book.'

'Wow, that's amazing,' said Camilla. 'I didn't know you could read.'

Just then there was a big cheer!

A group of children were diving off the pier into the sea.

They would

run,

and jump,

and land in the water with a big splash.

'Come and join us,' they called to Camilla. 'We're having lots of fun!'

'Oh, no thank you,' called Camilla. 'I don't go in the same water as Adidas swimwear.'

Thankfully, it wasn't long before Papa arrived with the yacht, and everyone stopped to admire it.

'Wow!' said one of the other children. 'Can we come aboard too, and play?'

'No,' said Camilla.

And they set sail for Capri.

Nanny's Day Off

———

'Oh golly,' said Astrid, jumping out of bed. 'I've overslept!'

It was 10am, and Astrid was late. She threw on some clothes, and pulled on some shoes, and hurried downstairs for breakfast.

'Astrid!' said Mama, putting down her martini.

'You're all back to front!'

She was right! Astrid was all in a muddle.

Her shoes were on the wrong feet,

her arms were in the wrong sleeves,

and her cardigan barely matched her Van Cleef & Arpels

bracelets. It was very embarrassing!

'Nanny usually dresses me,' said Astrid, 'but she wasn't there! And she didn't wake me up this morning, either.'

'Nanny has the day off today,' explained Mama. 'So you will have to do things for yourself.'

'That's fine' said Astrid. 'I don't need her. I'll make my own coffee.'

They looked at the coffee machine.

'One oat milk cortado, please,' said Astrid, hopefully.

The machine did NOT start.

'You're fired!' said Astrid, angrily.

Then it was time to take Aesop for a walk.

'Shall I wear a coat?' said Astrid.

'I don't know,' said Mama. 'What would Nanny say?'

'I think she would tell me to wear a coat,' said Astrid,

putting on her Canada Goose.

'I am *fucking boiling*,' said Astrid five minutes later,

as she walked along the street.

It was a very hot day.

Just then, a scary man appeared with a clipboard.

'Hello,' said the scary man. 'Would you like to sign our petition to Save The Children?'

'I'm sorry, Nanny usually talks to poor people for me!' said Astrid, spraying him with mace.

'Ahhhh,' said the man.

Back at home, Astrid and Mama were stressed.

Astrid needed to bring a cake to school – but Nanny

usually made their cakes!

'It doesn't have to be much,' fretted Astrid.

'Just a simple *Torta di Mele* or even a *Gâteau Basque*!'

They rummaged around in Nanny's cookbooks.

'How about this?' said Astrid, holding up a recipe.

'Oh yes, Nigella Lawson,' said Mama. 'She's **old**

money, we can trust her.'

They **stirred** and they **whipped,**

and **folded** and **sieved,**

and made an **almighty** mess.

Astrid even managed to dust the whole kitchen – and

Mama – with flour!

'Oh, it's just like the '80s...' said Mama, wiping her nose.

When they were finished, they admired their cake.

It was lumpy, and raw but also somehow burnt – and

a *very* strange colour.

'Perhaps I'll just buy a cake on the way to school,' said

Astrid, nervously.

'*Kill me,*' whispered the cake.

'Remember to tidy your room, Astrid,' called Papa, as Astrid went upstairs.

Astrid's room was *very* untidy. There were clothes everywhere, and assorted currency scattered across the floor, and her lacrosse sticks were tangled up in her loom.

'I think it will be easier to just start again,' sighed Astrid,

lighting a match.

At that moment, Nanny came through the door.

'Hello Astrid!' said Nanny. 'Your Mama called to say

you might need my help.'

'Nanny!' cried Astrid, throwing her arms around

her. 'Today has been awful without you!'

'Well, if you all need me so much,' chuckled Nanny,

'maybe I should finally get that raise!'

'Absolutely not,' smiled Astrid.

Bartie Goes Trick
or Treating

———

'Farewell, Mama', cried Bartie, pulling on a Schöffel gilet. **'IT'S HALLOWEEN!'**

'Mmmhmff,' said Mama,

who was having her fillers done.

Outside, the streets were full of fun. Everywhere, there were children dressed up in spooky outfits, like VAMPIRES and MIDDLE MANAGEMENT.

Bartie wandered down the road and met up with his good friends Sebastian and Shallotte.

'Have you got your pumpkin, Bartie?' they asked.

'Actually, this year I've gone for a kabocha squash,' he said, holding it up. 'I find it sweeter on the palate.'

'Trick or treat, Mrs Cheng,' shouted the children, knocking on the mansion next door.

'Hello children,' said Mrs Cheng, who was high on prescription medication. 'What have you come as?'

'I'm a **WIZARD!**' said Sebastian

'And I'm a **WEREWOLF!**' said Shallotte.

'And I'm **NOUVEAU RICHE**,' said Bartie.

'GASP,' said Mrs Cheng, crossing herself.

'That is *horrifying*, Bartie!'

And she gave them each a handful of Perello olives and an iPhone 16 Pro Max.

'What shall we do now?' wondered Shallotte, when they'd finished.

'How about Knock Door Run?' suggested Sebastian. 'We could knock on people's doors, and run away before they can answer!'

'We could,' said Bartie. 'But our driveways are just too long!'

'And our butlers are simply too fast,' agreed Shallotte.

In the end, they decided to snuggle up in their White Company blankets and watch something scary on TV – *Coronation Street.*

'People don't actually *live* like this, do they?'

said Shallotte, watching through her fingers.

'No, don't be silly,' chuckled Bartie. '**No one** could

live like this.'

And they drifted off to sleep.

David Upholsters a Chair

———

It was a bright sunny morning, and David was *busy*. He'd planted a clematis in his mindfulness garden, and been to reformer Pilates, then met Mama to brunch and bitch about Sandra's divorce.

David had a delicious shakshuka, whilst Mama enjoyed two pine nuts and a glass of wine.

'If Sandra simply got some more fillers, maybe then

she could hold down a man,' concluded David, kindly.

'Now farewell, Mama, I'm off to look at fabrics.'

'Uhurhuahuhrhhh,' slurred Mama.

David had *lots* of fun at the fabric shop.

'Wheeeeee!' he said, running his hands over the Egyptian cottons.

'Hello lad. D'you need any 'elp selectin' a fabric?' asked the shopkeeper, who was from a country called 'Yorkshire'.

'I'm sorry, I don't understand,' said David, nervously.

'Do you need any help selecting a fabric?' the shopkeeper said again.

'Not a word,' said David, sadly.

In the end, he selected a fine Liberty print, then headed back home to upholster a chair.

His friend Timothée even came round to help!

They had a wonderful time **cutting** the silks and **stapling** the wood, then took a short break to share one of Mama's pills.

'Reminds me of that time in Palm Springs,' said Timothée, taking another glass of champagne from Nanny 4.

When they were finished, they stood back to admire

their work.

'It's serving mid-century!' said Timothée.

'Indeed,' David agreed.

He smiled. If there was one thing in life that every

seven-year-old boy should take pride in, he thought,

it was **soft furnishings**.

Percy Goes to Slough

——

'All aboard,' cried Mrs Bodlean CBE. 'Everybody take a seat!'

It was a bright summer's day, and the children were going on a school trip. Percy was very excited.

He had packed his lunch box, and his camera, and he was ready for an adventure.

'Today we are going to a place called "**Slough**",'

said Mrs Bodlean CBE once they were on the coach.

'So that we can learn about cultures that are very, very

different from ours.'

'My mummy says we shouldn't be going to Slough,'

said a little girl. 'She says it's far too dangerous!'

'Don't be SILLY,' said Percy. '*My* mummy says *everyone*

should go to Slough – so that we know how truly, truly

lucky we all are.'

When they arrived in Slough, Mrs Bodlean CBE gave

them each a clipboard and some pencils.

'Take lots of **notes** and **pictures** of what you see,'
she said. 'But REMEMBER: be back at the coach by
two o'clock, or we shall leave you **behind**.' And with
that, she went off to have an affair with the coach driver.

The children were *very* excited to explore Slough.
They walked in groups of four, taking notes of all the
things they spotted.

Percy took lots of photos!

He took a photo of a woman in a bin.

He took a photo of a Betfred.

He took a photo of a mattress.

Then they stopped to have some lunch.

However, just as Percy was about to tuck in, a seagull

flew down and **snatched** his sandwich!

'Oh no!' said Percy. 'My quail's egg tartine!'

'You'll have to buy something new for lunch, Percy!' said his

friend Perinea. 'Why don't we go to that Little Waitrose?'

They crossed the road and headed into the shop.

There were sandwiches and crisps, but there were also things called 'scratchcards' and 'vapes'.

'This isn't like any Little Waitrose I've been in,' said Percy, nervously.

'Oh no, this isn't a Waitrose,' said a man behind the counter. 'This is a "Corner Shop"!'

Once they'd stopped running, the children examined their notes.

'We're supposed to write down an example of *local cuisine*,' said Percy. 'Maybe we could find somewhere to have a coffee?'

'That's a good idea,' said Michaelmas. 'I'm *dying* for a flat white.'

They looked and looked and looked, but they simply couldn't find a coffee house! They were about to give up when Percy spotted a sign.

'Look there!' he said, pointing. 'There's a cafe on the other side of the road.'

'Oh, but it's a Costa,' said Perinea, sadly.

'Are we in hell?!' said Michaelmas.

Whilst they all stood around drawing the Costa on their sketchpads, a man approached them.

'Hello you lot, what are you doing here then?' said the man. 'A school trip, is it?'

The children FROZE.

'Do you need any directions?' asked the man.

'*Don't move,*' whispered Percy. '*They can't see you if you don't move.*'

The children stayed perfectly still for what seemed like **hours,** and eventually the man walked away.

They had stopped for so long that it was almost **two o'clock!** They ran all the way back to the coach and got there just in the nick of time.

'Hurry along, children,' said Mrs Bodlean CBE. 'We were just about to leave you in this *accursed place*!'

Percy sighed in relief as they set off back for Richmond.

That was *quite enough* Slough for one lifetime.

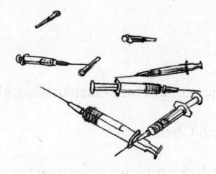

Penelope's Night Before Christmas

———

'Twas the night before Christmas, and all through Chelsea

The maids were still cleaning for a nominal fee.

The stockings were hung by Nanny 3 with care,

And Papa was conducting a sordid affair.

The children were dressed in their crushed-silk pyjamas,

That Mama had purchased whilst in the Bahamas.

But when Mama took a valium and fell asleep in her chair,

Her daughter Penelope snuck down the stairs…

She had heard on the roof a most curious clatter,

As if one of her ponies had climbed up a ladder.

So she crept to the landing for a better view

When from the dining hall came a **crash**, and a jingling too...

Peeking inside, she gasped there to see

A man all in red and white burst from the chimney.

'Oh my gosh,' she exclaimed, taking in his fur parka,

'I'm sorry, your coat... is it Balenciaga?'

He chuckled and nodded, his laugh sweet as honey,

And Penelope relaxed: he was clearly from money.

'But where have you come from?' Penelope cried,

And he showed her his satchel with presents inside.

'From a magical place,' he said, eyes like fires,

'Where one can find all that one's true heart desires.'

'Do you mean Selfridges?' asked Penelope.

And he nodded, and smiled, and her heart sang with glee.

Then he sprang to his feet, and she hugged him goodbye,

And back up the chimney he swiftly did fly —

To the roof, where his sleigh and his reindeer were reined.

And she heard, as they took off, him call out their names:

'NOW WAITROSE, NOW BODEN,

NOW NIGELLA LAWSON,

ON HARVEY NICKS, PRADA,

ON ALL-BUTTER CROISSANT,

To the top of the mansion, to the top of wall,

Now dash away, dash away, dash away all!'

They sped through the air like a Range Rover Evoque,
Higher than chimneys, higher than smoke,

And as Penelope rushed back inside, she realised,

quick as a flash,

He had given her all she truly needed –

£60,000 hard cash.

Wilfred's New Year's Eve

───

'Look, look!' cried Wilfred. 'The fireworks are starting! Let's go and watch.'

It was New Year's Eve, and everyone was having a *wonderful* time. Papa was smoking a cigar and saying something problematic, and Mama was getting drunk and causing a scene, whilst Wilfred and the other children played fun New Year's games!

'That one looks like a flower!' said Damson.

'That one looks like a Pollock!' said Raclette.

'And *that* one looks like my coat of arms!' said Wilfred.

'There you are, Master Wilfred,' said Butler, holding

the champagne. 'Do you and your friends need a drink?'

'We can't drink champagne, Butler!' chuckled

Wilfred. 'We're only nine! We'll just have a round

of gin and tonics.'

'Of course, Master Wilfred,' said Butler.

The party was a big success. There was **dancing** and **music**, and then everyone played charades.

'What am I?' said Papa, waving his hands and pulling a silly face.

'Oh, oh, I know!' said Mama. 'You're *"austerity"*!'

Then Wilfred read out one of his poems. Everyone thought it was *very good*.

'That was excellent, Wilfred,' said Richard Branson.

'*Good show, old boy,*' said The Rt Hon Grandpapa.

'I didn't know you could speak Aramaic!' said Damson.

When midnight grew near, they all raised their glasses and counted down the seconds. But Wilfred had no one to kiss!

Ten... nine... eight...

He looked at Damson, but she was with Raclette.

Seven... six... five...

He looked at Mama, but she was with her tennis coach.

Four... three... two...

He looked at Papa, but he was already kissing

a photograph of Margaret Thatcher.

One!

At that moment Nanny 2 appeared and gave him a **big kiss** on the cheek. Then they all cheered and sang a silly song.

'Happy New Year, Wilfred!' said Nanny 2.

'Happy New Year,' said Wilfred.

'Do you have any resolutions?' she asked.

'Just the usual, I think,' said Wilfred, thoughtfully.

'Lose 10 lbs and diversify my portfolio.'

'I think I'm going to read more,' said Nanny 2, smiling.

'That's great!' said Wilfred, rubbing his cheek. 'You can

start by reading your P45 in the morning.'

And he went to recite another poem.

Tammy Survives
the Apocalypse

———

'Wake up, Tammy,' said Papa, calling up the Grade II listed staircase.

'It's the apocalypse!'

'Coming Papa,' said Tammy, putting on her Olivia von Halle pyjamas.

The country was on fire, and *everyone* was very busy!

Nanny 4 was packing Tammy's shoes and Mama

was drinking wine, whilst Butler bailed seawater out

of a second-floor window.

'Make sure you don't get any brine on those Cézannes,'

suggested Tammy, helpfully. 'You'll damage the

varnish.'

Papa was *very* grumpy, because his collection of classic

cars had melted.

'This is because people didn't recycle their yoghurt

pots!' moaned Papa, who owned shares in oil and gas.

Then things got even worse! At lunchtime, the kitchen fell into a sinkhole, so there was nowhere for Chef to cook.

'What will we have for lunch now?' cried Tammy.

'We shall have to eat leftovers,' said Mama.

'Gosh, I didn't know you *could* eat food from yesterday,' said Tammy, nibbling a piece of cheese. 'How avant-garde!'

After lunch, Tammy was *very* organised. She wrapped up the Rothkos and helped Papa count the bullion, then sorted her clothing for the BIG TRIP.

'Which of these says "Mars" to you?' she asked, holding up two Moncler fleeces.

'Maybe pack both,' said Nanny 4. 'Then you have options.'

Tammy thought that was a **good idea.**

Before long, everything was packed and they were loading their things into the **Range Rover Escape Pod**.

'It's a good job Papa is friends with all those tech moguls,' chuckled Tammy, watching a school float down the street.

'Where shall I sit, Tammy?' said Nanny 4, passing them their suitcases.

'Hmm,' said Tammy, leaning on a desalination tank.

She looked at the **crates of wine,** and she looked at the **croquet mallets** and the **dog accessorie**s, and she looked at her **backup manicure station** – but she simply couldn't see *anything* they could leave behind!

'I'm sorry, it doesn't look like there's any room for you,' Tammy explained, kindly. 'But I'm sure you'll think of something!'

And they blasted off into the sky.